THE CAPTAIN'S MAP TO SUCCESS

A Navigational Guidebook For Your 12-Weeks to Success Program and Planner

Risen
LIFE COACHING

The Captain's Map to Success: A Navigational Guidebook For Your 12-Weeks to Success Program and Planner

Published by Dawn's New Light Publishing LLC.

Cover illustration designed with Canva

ISBN 979-8-218-36287-4

For more information visit:

risenlifecoaching.com

dawnrichey.com

associationofsoulsavers.org

To you the reader :

May you come to realize your true

potential and achieve the most

extraordinary dreams that reside

within you.

THE CAPTAIN'S MAP TO SUCCESS

A Navigational Guidebook
For Your
12-Weeks to Success
Program and Planner

PLANNING BELIEVING ACHIEVING

Dawn's New Light
Publishing LLC

Congratulations!

You have officially embarked on the initial significant step towards realizing all your wonderful goals. Your commitment to this 12-Week Program has propelled you much closer to the life you've always envisioned.

The most exciting aspect is that by following these steps as outlined, and recording them consistently in your planner, you can be confident that you will undoubtedly taste the sweet success of accomplishing your goals!

TABLE OF CONTENTS

"Fix your course on a star and

you'll navigate every storm"

Leonardo da Vinci

YOUR JOURNEY BEGINS...

I magine yourself as the captain of a beautiful, pristine ship. Standing in the pilothouse after a long journey towards your destination, you finally catch sight of it. As you draw closer, a surge of excitement fills you. Your ship carries precious cargo poised to change the lives of thousands, perhaps millions of people. A smile graces your face at the thought of the joy they will soon experience once these goods reach their destination.

While your crew works diligently and happily to prepare for arrival, your gaze remains fixed on your destination. Your heart swells with gladness. It's been a challenging journey, but the rewards for your labor are on the horizon. After the obligatory celebration, you anticipate a rest like never before. With a deep, cleansing breath, you relish the moment. You've finally made it.

You
AS CAPTAIN

Similar to a captain who navigates with precise coordinates and a map to reach their destined ports, you, too, require the exact coordinates that will guide you toward your aspirations. Obtaining these coordinates involves vividly envisioning the grandest version of yourself, a decade and just twelve weeks from now.

It is imperative to craft a detailed vision of your distant future as it inherently shapes the objectives of the immediate 12 weeks, ensuring alignment and coherence between the two.

Close your eyes, take a deep breath in and allow the vision to become as clear as possible.

Take a poignant moment now, let your mind paint a vivid picture- how do you envision yourself looking, feeling, and thriving in a decade? Visualize this profound imagery akin to witnessing the pinnacle climax of your life projected on a cinematic screen before you.

Now, take a moment to envision yourself in the near future—12 weeks, or roughly 3 months, from this point. It's essential to strike a balance between ambition and pragmatism while visualizing this temporal horizon. Aim for considerable progress without drifting into overly ambitious territory.

Precise planning and unwavering commitment can yield substantial accomplishments within this 12-week span. So set your aspirations high, but with a keen eye on maintaining a realistic perspective. Setting goals that are overly ambitious might result in disillusionment and frustration. Strive to discover the 'Goldilocks zone'—a sweet spot that resonates perfectly with your capabilities and aspirations

Wonderful! You have just completed the first and most important part of your program. You are going to use these visions to help you obtain your coordinates and map out your plan for success.

"Visualize this thing that you want, see it, feel it, believe in it. Make your mental blueprint and begin to build"

-Robert Colier

How to Use
Your Planner

PLANNING BELIEVING
ACHIEVING

MONTH: _____

Sunday	Monday	Tuesday	Wednesday
		1	2
6	7	8	9
		Lunch with Jill	
13	14	15	16
	Dr Appt 8:00		
20	21	22	23
27	28	29	30

VAC

NOTES: _____

YEAR: _____

Thursday	Friday	Saturday
3	4	5
10	11	12
17	18	19
	Ivo's BDAY!	
24	25	26
31		

ATION

NOTES: _____ Take more naps
Make sure that the kids get to practice on time!

While there are many digital options to plan and organize your life, the act of physically writing things down creates a personal connection.

Seeing your own handwriting evokes a stronger sense of ownership and commitment to your goals and allows for more creativity and personalization. However, it can also be helpful to have certain important events inputted digitally so as to have reminders and notifications.

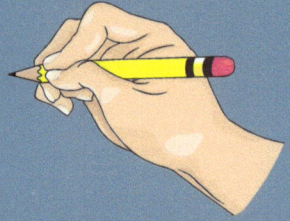

- Start by opening your planner and signing your name below where it says, "Property of Captain"

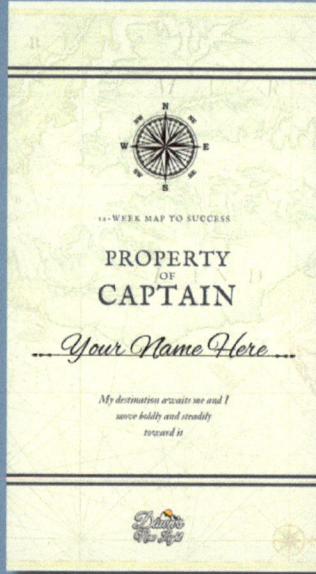

12-WEEK MAP TO SUCCESS

PROPERTY
OF
CAPTAIN

Your Name Here

My destination awaits me and I
move boldly and steadily
toward it

You have now taken the first TANGIBLE step toward achieving your success!

The
VISION BOARD

On the next two pages you will see an area purposed for gluing images similar to the ones you envisioned moments ago when you established your vision for the next 10 years as well as the next 12 weeks.

To create your vision board, follow these steps:

- Gather Materials: Collect magazines, printouts, images from the internet, scissors, glue, and your planner.

- Select Relevant Images: Look for pictures that resonate with your visions for the next 10 years and the upcoming 12 weeks. Focus on choosing images that reflect the experiences you want to have, rather than material possessions like cars or objects—this helps align your goals with meaningful, lasting fulfillment and avoids unintended outcomes.

- Print or Cut: If you're using printed images, upload and print them. Otherwise, cut out the selected images from magazines or other sources.

- Arrange and Glue: Arrange the images on the designated area in your planner. Organize them in a way that is visually appealing and meaningful to you. Once satisfied with the arrangement, glue them onto the pages.

Example

Creating a vision board can indeed be seen as a meticulous task, yet its effectiveness in stimulating the subconscious mind towards manifesting desired outcomes is profound. Understanding that neglecting this step might compromise your success in achieving your goals emphasizes its importance. Viewing and engaging with your envisioned aspirations regularly can significantly influence your mindset and actions, fostering alignment with your desired future.

Your
Physical
Transformation

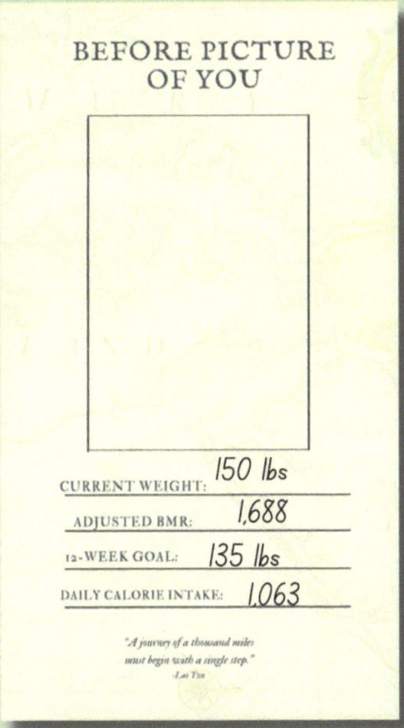

BEFORE PICTURE OF YOU

CURRENT WEIGHT: *150 lbs*

ADJUSTED BMR: *1,688*

12-WEEK GOAL: *135 lbs*

DAILY CALORIE INTAKE: *1,063*

"A journey of a thousand miles must begin with a single step."
-Lao Tzu

Example

Taking a "before" picture can be a motivating step in a fitness or personal improvement journey. It provides a visual baseline to track progress and serves as a reminder of where you started.

As you make progress towards your goals, comparing these photos over time can be incredibly inspiring and validating and can boost motivation. Remember, the primary goal is progress and improvement, so use these photos as a tool to stay motivated and track your journey.

• Take a moment to snap a photo of yourself in the mirror. What you are wearing is entirely up to you. Some people like to wear a minimal amount of clothing so as to see the greatest improvements in their physiques in the after picture, but whatever you feel comfortable wearing is best for you. Once you have taken the photo, have it printed out and paste it on the appointed page (note: while this portion of the program can be helpful and motivating, it is optional).

• If, in this program, you are looking to achieve a slimmer physique, the following steps are a fail-proof way to reach your weight-loss goals. Start by entering your **Current Weight** on the appointed line in your planner (as pictured above).

- Now calculate your Basal Metabolic Rate (BMR) by following the steps below. Establishing a calorie deficit is pivotal in achieving your desired weight. Your BMR denotes the calories burned at rest to sustain essential bodily functions. To compute your BMR:

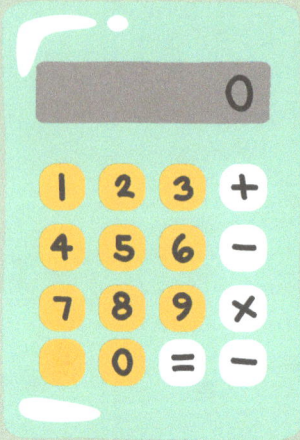

- **Convert Weight to Kilograms:** If accustomed to pounds, convert your weight to kilograms by dividing your weight in pounds by 2.205 [example: if your current weight is 150 lbs (150/2.205= 68 kilograms)]

- **Convert Height to Centimeters:** If height is in inches, multiply the number by 2.54 to obtain centimeters [example: if your height is 64 inches (64 x 2.54 = 162.56 centimeters)]

Once you have your weight in kilograms and height in centimeters, calculate your BMR using the Harris-Benedict equation:

- **For Men:** BMR = 88.362 + (13.397 × weight in kg) + (4.799 × height in cm) - (5.677 × age in years)

- **For Women:** BMR = 447.593 + (9.247 × weight in kg) + (3.098 × height in cm) - (4.330 × age in years)

[example if you are a 40-year-old woman:
447.593 + (9.247 x 68) + (3.098 x 162.56) - (4.330 x 40) =

1,407 calories burned per day at rest (BMR)]

- **Estimate Daily Calorie Needs:** Now multiply your BMR by your daily activity factor (sedentary, lightly active, moderately active) to calculate the daily calorie intake needed to maintain your current weight. Then enter that number on the appointed line labeled **Adjusted BMR**

  -Sedentary: If you get minimal or no exercise, multiply your BMR by 1.2 (example: 1407 x 1.2 = 1,688 calories per day)

  -Lightly active: If you exercise lightly one to three days a week, multiply your BMR by 1.375 (example: 1407 x 1.375= 1,934 calories per day)

  -Moderately active: If you exercise moderately three to five days a week, multiply your BMR by 1.55 (example: 1407 x 1.55 = 2,180 calories per day)

- **Define your Goal Weight:** Set a realistic target weight to attain and enter it on the appointed line labeled **12-Week Goal** in your planner beneath the Before Picture of You.

- **Determine your Calorie Deficit:** Firstly, it is important to note that one pound of fat is equal to 3,500 calories. So subtract your 12-week Goal weight from your current weight and multiply that number by 3,500 [example: if your current weight is 150 lbs. and your goal is 135 lbs (a difference of 15 lbs), you will multiply 3,500 by 15 to get 52,500 calories- this is the total number of calories you will need to burn in 12 weeks to reach your goal]

  - Now divide that number by 12
  (ex. 52,500/ 12 = 4375 calories per week)

  - Now divide that number by 7 to obtain your
  Daily Calorie Deficit (ex. 4,375/ 7 = 625 calories less per day)

- Finally, subtract your Daily Calorie Deficit from your Adjusted BMR to obtain your **Daily Calorie Intake** and input this number on the appointed line in your planner beneath the Before Picture of You (example: 1,688 - 625 = **1,063 calories per day**)

If you consume your calculated Daily Calorie Intake every day for 12 weeks, you will, without a doubt, reach your weight loss goal! Remember that goal will be reached without even changing your daily activity level. However, if you increase your activity level, you can add more calories to your daily intake or you can decrease the time it takes to reach your goal.

Many calorie-specific diets can be found online, making planning your meals easier. Otherwise, you can obtain a calorie counting book and calculate your daily calories that way. Essentially, the goal is to burn more calories than you consume.

It is important not to obsess with calorie consumption however and allow yourself to occasionally indulge in your favorite foods and treats (after all, enjoying a delicious meal and tasty treat helps make life pleasurable). You can also find a weight-loss-specific hypnosis program along with a calorie-specific diet on the website that will help you acquire a healthy mindset geared toward exercise motivation and appetite regulation. Click on the QR code below for more information.

While this approach to weight loss has proven to be safe and effective for most, it is recommended that you consult your physician to be sure it is right for you.

- After you have completed the program, take another picture of yourself wearing the same outfit, or a similar one, and paste it on the appointed page in your planner labeled "After Picture of You" and note your final weight on the appointed line below the picture.

THE MISSION STATEMENT

Crafting a mission statement is a crucial step in defining your values and guiding principles. It serves as a compass for your actions and decisions, aligning with your aspirations and beliefs. Here are steps to help you create a meaningful mission statement:

- Reflect on Core Values: Consider your personal values, beliefs, and aspirations. What principles are fundamental to you? What drives you towards your goals?

- Keep it Concise and Clear: A good mission statement is succinct and easily understandable. It should reflect your purpose and intentions crisply and clearly.

- Consider Impact and Purpose: Think about the impact you wish to have and the purpose behind your actions. How do you want to contribute or make a difference?

- Write and Revise: Start by jotting down ideas on a piece of paper. Refine and revise your statements until you have a version that resonates deeply with you.

- Review and Finalize: Once you've refined your mission statement, review it thoroughly. Ensure it encapsulates your values and goals accurately.

- Record it in Your Planner: When you're satisfied with your mission statement, write it down in your planner (preferably in long-hand) where you'll see it regularly.

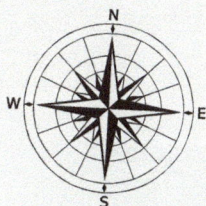

MISSION STATEMENT

To manifest divine visions with unwavering faith, disciplined effort, organization, and consistency creating abundant benefits for myself and others.

"Fix your course on a star and you'll navigate every storm."
-Napoleon Hill

Example

Your
10-YEAR DESTINATION

10-YEAR DESTINATION

I will be the head of a global enterprise with many passive income generating businesses with at least $ 10 million in the bank. I will be healthy, attractive, happily married, have all my kids in college, and will be charitable with my time and finances.

"Have the end in mind and every day make sure you're working towards it."
- Ryan Allis

Example

Reminding yourself daily of where you aspire to be in 10 years, is a powerful way to set your course and maintain focus on your ultimate goals. This consistent reflection allows you to reinforce your long-term vision, keeping it at the forefront of your mind. By vividly imagining your desired future on a daily basis, you solidify your intentions, align your actions with your aspirations, and stay motivated on the path towards achieving those long-term goals. Regularly revisiting and reaffirming this vision helps guide your decisions and actions, ensuring they are in harmony with your objectives.

Your
12-WEEK DESTINATION

Maintaining a clear vision of your destination for the upcoming 12 weeks is crucial for staying focused and committed to your short-term goals. Reading this vision aloud daily reinforces your commitment and keeps your objectives at the forefront of your mind.

12-WEEK DESTINATION

I will lose 15 pounds and tone-up and will joyfully engage in a regular fitness routine. I will write an inspiring book to help others overcome depression and also teach a seminar. I will celebrate by taking my family on a cruise.

"Believe in your infinite potential. Your only limitations are those you set upon yourself."
- Roy T. Bennett

Example

YOUR PAST VICTORIES

One of the most powerful tools we have in our journey to success is our own history. Each of us has overcome unique challenges, achieved milestones, and experienced moments of victory, no matter how big or small. Rememberin and reflecting on these past accomplishments isn't just an exercise in nostalgia; it's a way to harness the momentum of past victories to fuel our current journey. Reflecting on past victories also helps to shift our mindset. This isn't about resting on our laurels; it's about using those victories as stepping stones, evidence that you can tackle whatever challenges lie ahead.

In your planner, there's a dedicated area for listing some of your most remarkable past accomplishments. Take time to reflect deeply on this portion. Your accomplishments might include moments of overcoming emotional obstacles, achieving professional feats, and significant acquisitions or milestones. This list is not just a record; it's a personal testament to your resilience and strength. By documenting these victories, you're creating a powerful resource that you can revisit whenever you need a reminder of your capability.

PAST ACCOMPLISHMENTS

- Bought my house

- Overcame my fear of public speaking

- started a cleaning business

- Paid off my car

"Acknowledge all of your small victories. They will eventually add up to something great."
- Kara Goucher

Example

THE VARIOUS ROLES

The holistic nature of the "12 Weeks to Success" program emphasizes that success encompasses various facets of life, not just one particular area.

It's vital to pay attention to your physical health, mental and spiritual well-being, relationships, personal development, and other significant areas alongside your defined goals. In order to address all these areas, they have been categorized (in the nautical appropriate theme ;) on the following pages.

The CAPTAIN

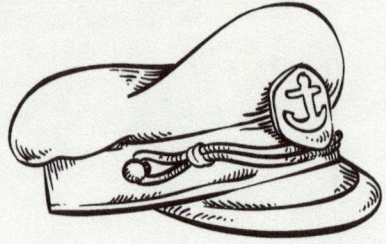

The Captain represents your spirit and your mind. Just as the captain governs the activities of the vessel and the crew, the spirit governs the mind and the mind governs your body and actions.

Some examples of ways you can improve the captain's role might be: prayer, meditation, going to church, reading/ listening to enriching literature, playing challenging puzzles, playing music, seeking the council of a therapist, and spending time in nature.

The VESSEL

The vessel represents your body and other aspects of your life that provide sustainability (including your day-job).

Some examples of improving the role of the vessel include: physical exercise, eating nutritious foods, eliminating harmful foods and substances, getting a massage, getting proper rest, and going to work.

The
CREW

The crew represents your interpersonal relationships-those closest to you who rely on you and whom you also rely on to navigate your way through life.

Ways you can improve your relationships with your crew: going on dates with your spouse or partner, doing homework with your child, playing sports or games with your child, calling your friends/ family members, and asking your boss if they need any extra help.

The PORTMEN

Though this is an archaic term, *Portmen* refer to a group of citizens of a port or town responsible for the town's affairs. In this program, the portmen represent the target audience you want to reach with the goods or services you are offering. It also represents the people who can benefit from your charitable services. Sharing your precious time, energy, and sustenance with those in need may be the most fulfilling actions we can take in life.

Examples of improving the role of the portmen might include: advertising your product/ services/ talents on social media, sending individual messages to people who might be interested in what you have to offer, signing up to give a lecture,
serving at your local homeless shelter, serving at your church, or visiting with lonely individuals who are in restricted facilities.

The Power of
SUBCONSCIOUS
THERAPY

Subconscious therapy is a safe and very effective transformative modality, wielding the ability to propel you toward your aspirations. By dismantling self-imposed limitations, it becomes a guiding force in cultivating a robust and wholesome mindset, fostering not just healing but also motivation on your journey to success. Click on the link below to learn more.

Risen

LIFE COACHING

PORTS OF CALL

The "Ports of Call" symbolize the diverse array of objectives you aim to achieve, serving as pivotal milestones guiding you toward your ultimate 12-week destination.

Your pursuits may encompass an assortment of smaller yet distinct goals or be directed toward a singular significant objective. In either scenario, these seven distinct ports serve as the intermediary checkpoints, each essential in navigating the path toward accomplishing the ultimate goal which in this case is your 12-week destination.

- Dedicate time to ponder the sequential steps necessary to attain your goal, as they will collectively compose your indispensable "nautical chart" or "map." Researching individuals who have successfully navigated a comparable path can offer invaluable insights into the actions and strategies that will help pave the way for your success.

- When you feel confident in the smaller goals or steps you must take, label them in sequential order on the map.

- Although not necessary, making your first port targeted to a health and fitness regimen is encouraged as optimal physical and mental health will substantially increase your focus, efficiency, and confidence, making it easier to reach all of your goals.

- While some choose to complete one goal before moving to the next, others prefer to "circumnavigate" by working a little bit on each goal until they are all completed and the final destination is reached. Whichever path you choose is right for you.

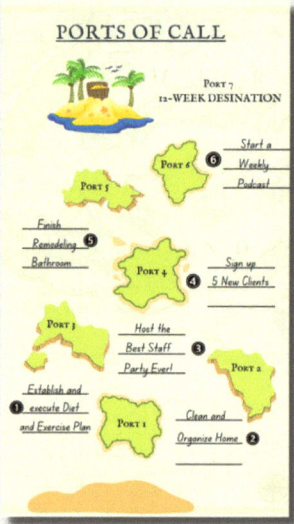

Example of map with
several smaller goals

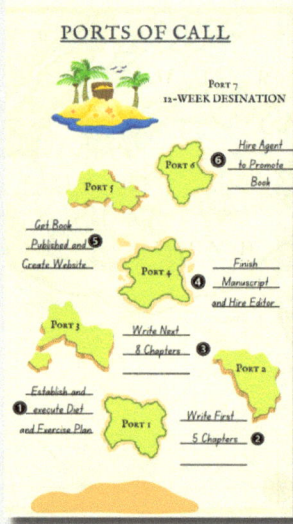

Example of map with one big goal
broken down into smaller parts

You can also schedule an appointment with one of our life coaches who can talk to you about your goals and help you map out your plan for success. Click the QR code for more information.

- On the following pages, allocate labels to each port and subsequently describe the emotions you will feel upon reaching these milestones. Engaging deeply with these emotions, even though they may not presently exist as tangible realities, can aid your subconscious mind in accepting them as actual possibilities. By immersing yourself in these emotional states associated with success and accomplishment, you create a mental environment that facilitates the acceptance of these emotions as plausible outcomes.

- This mental shift can attract and align your focus toward the means necessary to transform these emotional aspirations into tangible realities. Through this approach, you can harness the power of positive visualization and intention-setting to attract the resources, opportunities, and pathways that lead to realizing these desired emotional states and, consequently, your goals.

- Now, list the value actions necessary to reach your goals and arrive at your "Ports of Call". These actions will be used to help complete your "Prosperity Ledger" located in the Daily Planner section.

PORT I
Establish and Execute a Diet and Exercise Plan

HOW I WILL FEEL WHEN I ARRIVE AT THIS PORT:

I will feel healthy, attractive, young, full of energy, confident and motivated to pursue my goals with vigor.

✳

VALUE ACTIONS THAT WILL LEAD ME TO THIS PORT:

jog around block	work with a personal trainer
take supplements	make a diet plan
refrain from sodas	refrain from fast food
meal prep	

"There are no secrets to success. It is the result of preparation, hard work, and learning from failure."
-Colin Powell

Example

PORT II
Clean and Organize Home

HOW I WILL FEEL WHEN I ARRIVE AT THIS PORT:

I will feel clean, organized, and in control

✳

VALUE ACTIONS THAT WILL LEAD ME TO THIS PORT:

purchase cleaning products	get help
organize garage	take stuff to thrift store
clean out cabinets	fix vacuum cleaner
hire window cleaner	

"Some people want it to happen, some wish it would happen, others make it happen."
-Michael Jordan

Example

Pause for a moment and take a deep breath....

You're on the verge of completing the meticulous mapping of your plan! Before you know it, you will be savoring the sweet taste of success!

THE PROSPERITY BANK

The Prosperity Bank is a highly effective system inspired by Dr. John G. Kappas' Mental Bank Program. This program was specifically crafted to foster a mindset geared toward financial abundance, consequently attracting opportunities for its realization. Dr. Kappas, after experimenting with various methods aimed at shifting people away from a state of lack, discovered that the combination of symbolic language, ideomotor responses, and nightly reinforcement just before bedtime had the capacity to profoundly reprogram the subconscious. This reprogramming facilitated the attraction of financial abundance while dispelling a poverty mindset.

Similar to Dr. Kappas' approach, the Prosperity Bank operates on a parallel principle, proving to be effective not only in acquiring financial abundance but also in effortlessly and efficiently achieving all of your goals while simultaneously relinquishing unhealthy habits and adopting healthy ones. Before the instructions for completing this portion of the program are revealed, it is crucial to comprehend the significance of your subconscious mind in determining your overall level of success.

The
SUBCONSCIOUS MIND

From birth until the age of 12-years-old, our personality is believed to be 95% formed, influenced not only by genetics but significantly shaped by our experiences and everything we've been *programmed* to believe about ourselves and the world around us.

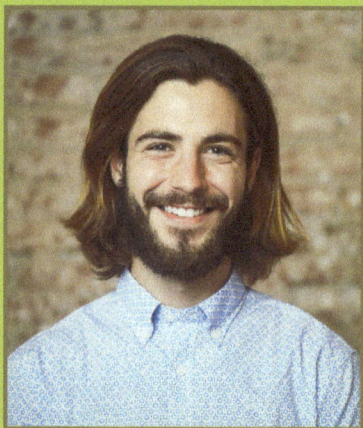

As we grow older, we tend to accept thoughts or ideas that only align with our existing *programming*, rejecting anything unfamiliar. Consequently, we develop a subconscious homeostasis, or the innate drive to stay the same.

Homeostasis functions like a thermostat. When the air inside your home becomes excessively warm, the thermostat activates the air conditioner to regulate the temperature according to its programmed settings. Perhaps more appropriately, it's comparable to the autopilot system on a ship. If the vessel deviates from its programmed coordinates, the autopilot takes charge of the steering gear, adjusting the rudder to guide the ship back onto its intended course.

Similar to the functioning of a thermostat or autopilot, when our subconscious mind encounters new ideas or experiences that differ from the established programming from early life, it tends to reject these ideas or may even alter the experiences to fit in line with the pre-existing programming. Keeping us in our "comfort zones" so to speak. Although this mechanism can be advantageous in maintaining stability, it becomes detrimental when one endeavors to make significant changes in life or aims to achieve ambitious goals.

"Reprogramming your subconscious mind is crucial for conquering a self-defeating mindset and evolving into the optimal version of yourself."

Consider an individual raised in poverty, where that circumstance defined their reality. They may instinctively resist the concept of living a life of luxury or even achieving financial stability. Such a person might feel inferior in comparison to those who enjoy financial prosperity and might even hold resentment toward them. Yet, the truth remains that they possess the capability to live a similar lifestyle if only their subconscious would accept such a truth.

It is necessary to break the subconscious homeostasis that is prohibiting you from attracting the resources and opportunities necessary to reach your goals. Reprogramming your subconscious mind is crucial for conquering a self-defeating mindset and evolving into the optimal version of yourself. Hence, the effectiveness of the Prosperity Bank lies in its ability to address and alter these ingrained perceptions and limitations, facilitating a transformation towards a more prosperous mindset. The outcomes might not materialize rapidly, but they will assuredly be achieved with persistence and dedication to the process.

It is also important to note that 88% of the time, we are functioning at a subconscious level. For instance, when you are driving, you are not consciously focusing on the gas pedal or the brakes, you are likely thinking about the concerns of your day. Your brain has been programmed to operate the vehicle subconsciously. Such is the case for most activities throughout your day. The subconscious mind doesn't inherently differentiate between reality and imagination. However, it consistently treats numbers and symbols as concrete and real elements. For this reason, the Prosperity Bank is a potent modality in dispelling a poverty mindset and attracting financial abundance.

The Prosperity Bank Contract

Now that you understand how the subconscious mind works and that it will *always* achieve what it is programmed for, you will have a better understanding of how and why the Prosperity Bank Program is so effective.

- Start by turning to the page in your planner entitled *Prosperity Contract* and write your name and put the date in the appropriate spaces (refer to the example)

- To the best of your ability, determine your annual income and double it then write that figure in the next space. This is your Prosperity Bank Goal. It is only 2 times your current income because it is reasonable and achievable, if you push for too much, your subconscious mind may not accept it. When you achieve that goal, you can double it again (if you don't have an annual income, enter $30,000).

PROSPERITY CONTRACT

I *Your Name Here* agree on this date of _____ *Todays Date* , to write my prosperity script to arrive at a yearly income of _____ *$100,000* . This amount will represent 25% of my Prosperity Bank balance which will be *$400,000* . I will arrive at this amount by paying myself a base amount of *$100* per hour for value actions that will lead me to my ports of call.

X *Your Signature Here*

Example

- Now, multiply your Prosperity Bank Goal by four and enter that amount in the provided space. This represents your Prosperity Bank Balance. Achieving this imaginary sum may very well align with reaching your Prosperity Bank Goal in reality!

- In this program you are both the employer and the employee and you pay yourself at an hourly rate for the value actions that are going to lead you to your goals. Your hourly rate is one thousandth of your Prosperity Bank Goal (refer to the example).

- Finally, sign your name at the bottom.

THE PROSPERITY BANK LEDGER

Consistently filling out the Prosperity Ledger every night before bedtime will emerge as your most potent tool for achieving your goals. This practice not only combines symbolic language with ideomotor responses at a time when they are embedded most effectively in your subconscious mind but also reinforces the powerful practice of consistency, an essential element in attaining any goal.

Example

Date: Today's Date			Goal: $100.000	

PROSPERITY LEDGER

Value Activity	Price Per Hour	Hours Performed	Daily Total	Balance
Filled out ledger	100	-	100	950
exercised	100	2	200	1.150
got headshots	100	-	100	1.250
worked on book	200	3	600	1.850
advertised on IG	100	1	100	1.950
played soccer with Aden	100	1	100	2.050
did not use swear words	200	-	200	2.250
worked at job	100	8	800	3.050
			Minus Actual Money Earned	400
			Total Balance	2.650

As of this date, I have earned a balance of two thousand six hundred fifty dollars. I am moving boldly and steadily toward my goal.

x *Your Signature Here*

Notes:
I had a dream last night that I climbed to the top of a big mountain and looked out and saw the entire city! Everyone could see me too. They were waving.

Example

- The Prosperity Ledger is located in the Daily Planner portion of your planner. Begin by writing the date and your Prosperity Bank Goal at the top of the page as displayed in the example. Consistently writing and seeing your goal will yield a powerful response in your subconscious and consequently your reality.

- Under "Value Activity" write down any of your value actions that you worked on that day (these were input previously when you established your Ports of Call- you could input a maximum of 8). Include any activities centered around your various roles regarding the Captain, Vessel, Crew, and Portmen making sure to also include any hours worked at your day job. Additionally, add bad habits that you were able to refrain from that day paying yourself double the hourly rate for this accomplishment. Be sure to include "filled out ledger" as this is a very important step to achieving your goals.

- Under "Price Per Hour" add the hourly rate for each activity (one thousandth of your goal). For the more difficult or substantial activities, pay yourself twice the hourly rate.

- Under "Hours Performed" input the number of hours spent working on each activity. For activities that are minimal or less than an hour, you will pay yourself the flat hourly rate and input "na" or simply input a dash.

- Add the total amount you earned for each activity and input figure under "Daily Total"

- After figuring out your Daily Total, enter the balance in the last row on the right. The balance will always be the sum total. For the first entry in the Balance box on any new ledger, be sure to add the previous ledger's Total Balance (see example below)

- The most confusing step when filling out the Prosperity Ledger is filling in the "Minus Actual Money Earned" box. Many believe that giving away money is considered a loss, but in actuality, it is necessary in order to have it returned to you. Most people are reluctant to let go of their finances because they don't want to believe that they'll always have more. This is called *scarcity mentality*. In the case of the Prosperity Ledger however, the more money you are subtracting in that box, the more money you are actually making in reality. You will *want* to subtract money. It is truly a brilliant way to program the subconscious mind to overcome the scarcity mentality and must again be accredited to Dr. John G. Kappas.

- The final step of the Prosperity Ledger is handwriting this statement and following it with your signature:

    "As of this date, I have earned a balance of (your total balance written out). I am moving boldy and steadily toward my goal."

    x Your Signature.

- You will find a space at the bottom of the page to notate any significant thoughts or occurrences that took place each day

While the results of this program might not immediately reflect in your actual bank account within the initial 12-week period, rest assured that faithfully completing your ledger each night will significantly propel you toward, if not beyond, your Prosperity Bank goal shortly thereafter. Simultaneously, it will guide you to achieve all of your Ports of Call (within the 12 weeks) and, in due time, reach your ultimate destination. Additionally, you can acquire additional inserts after the 12-week period and continue this program indefinitely.

DATE: Today's Date   GOAL: $100.000

PROSPERITY LEDGER

Value Activity	Price Per Hour	Hours Performed	Daily Total	Balance
filled out ledger	100	–	100	2.750
exercised	100	2	200	2.950
worked on book	200	3	600	3.550
advertised on IG	100	1	100	3.650
did not drink soda	200	–	200	3.850
worked at day job	100	8	800	4.650

	Minus Actual Money Earned	0
	Total Balance	4.650

As of this date, I have earned a balance of four thousand six hundred fifty dollars. I am moving boldly and steadily toward my goal.

x *Your Signature Here*

NOTES:
Today was a good day. I broke my record time jogging around the block - 5 minutes 28 seconds! I was very productive.

Example

The half-hour before you go to bed is called the "magic half-hour" because whatever you feed your mind before bed will make its way into your dreams and into your subconscious. This is why it's important to complete your ledger at this time to acheive the maximum results. Also, be careful to not to feed your mind with anything negative before bed.

CIRCADIAN RHYTHMS

Before planning your months, weeks, and days, it's crucial to consider your body's circadian rhythms. These rhythms encompass the mental, physical, and behavioral changes experienced by nearly all living organisms in a 24-hour cycle. Often likened to biological clocks, they are primarily influenced by light and darkness, yet factors like stress, food intake, physical activity, temperature, and social environments also exert an impact.

Naturally, our circadian rhythms operate with remarkable consistency and, if undisturbed, promote good mental and physical health. However, disruptions to these rhythms can result in various health complications, including sleep deprivation, difficulty concentrating, obesity, diabetes, impaired digestion, blood pressure irregularities, and even an increased risk of cancer. Common disruptions stem from activities like traveling, late-night exposure to electronic devices, neurological disorders, and mental fatigue.

While our rhythms are fundamentally similar, they can diverge based on our genetic makeup and work schedules (for instance, individuals working graveyard shifts develop distinct circadian rhythms). Considering your circadian rhythms when planning daily activities proves beneficial. For instance, most individuals experience heightened alertness around 10 am, making mornings an ideal time for engaging in creative pursuits such as writing. While afternoons prove to be the best time for physical activities as our muscle strength, cardiovascular efficiency and coordination are at their peaks.

Have you ever experienced writer's block? You may have been trying to write during a time that was out-of-sync with your circadian rhythms.
Keep the rhythm and you will maintain efficiency and good health!

CIRCADIAN RHYTHMS

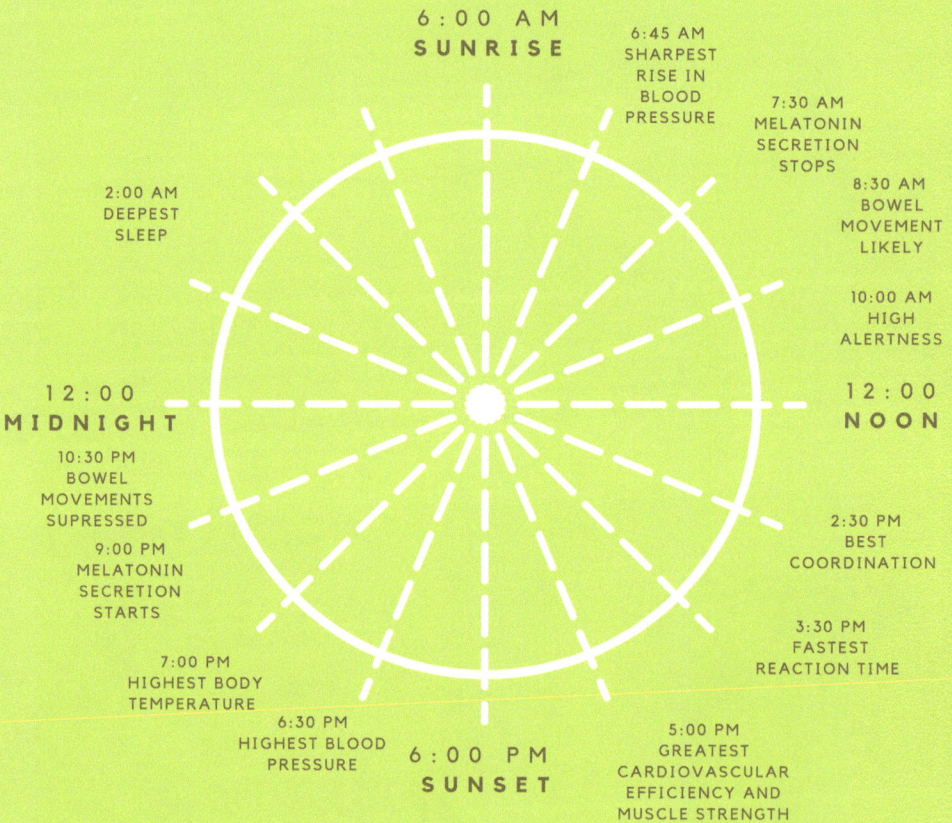

6:00 AM
SUNRISE

6:45 AM
SHARPEST
RISE IN
BLOOD
PRESSURE

7:30 AM
MELATONIN
SECRETION
STOPS

8:30 AM
BOWEL
MOVEMENT
LIKELY

10:00 AM
HIGH
ALERTNESS

2:00 AM
DEEPEST
SLEEP

12:00
MIDNIGHT

12:00
NOON

10:30 PM
BOWEL
MOVEMENTS
SUPRESSED

9:00 PM
MELATONIN
SECRETION
STARTS

2:30 PM
BEST
COORDINATION

3:30 PM
FASTEST
REACTION TIME

7:00 PM
HIGHEST BODY
TEMPERATURE

6:30 PM
HIGHEST BLOOD
PRESSURE

6:00 PM
SUNSET

5:00 PM
GREATEST
CARDIOVASCULAR
EFFICIENCY AND
MUSCLE STRENGTH

MONTHLY
EXPENSES

Maintaining a clear overview of your monthly expenses is crucial for success, particularly when working with limited funds. This dedicated page is designed to assist you in staying organized and maintaining control over your finances.

- List every expense that you are responsible for each month under the row entitled "Expense Name" and try to group them according business, home, and personal expenses

- In the next column, enter the date the expense is due or when it is drafted out of your account (you may also choose to include these on the monthly calendar or in your digital device)

- Under the row entitled "Contact" enter the contact information for each expense so you can get in touch with them in case of an emergency

- In the next column, enter the exact amount or approximate amount of each expense

- In the bottom of the chart, enter the total amount of all your monthly expenses

- Try to set aside a weekly amount for your savings (or perhaps for a special celebration once you've reached your final destination :) and write that amount in the appointed space

MONTHLY EXPENSES

	Expense	Due Date	Contact	Amount
BUSINESS	Social Promo	3rd	gosocail.com	18.00
	Google Wksp	4th	google.com	25.00
	Canva	21st	canva.com	15.00
HOME	Mortgage	1st	888-348-1234	2,200.00
	Water	21st	888-348-1234	~ 50.00
	Electric	15th	888-348-1234	~ 150.00
	Sewer	4th	888-348-1234	~ 40.00
	Internet	5th	888-348-1234	75.00
PERSONAL	Car	12th	888-348-1234	300.00
	Capital One	15th	888-348-1234	60.00
	Bank Loan	10th	888-348-1234	200.00
	Phone	10th	888-348-1234	90.00
			Total	**$3,223**

WEEKLY AMOUNT I WILL SET ASIDE

$80.00

The compact size of your planner was designed for convenient portability in your purse or other carrying devices. You will find that it is necessary to write small and to abbreviate when you can.

CREDIT AND DEBT

Establishing and sustaining good credit paves the way for numerous opportunities that might otherwise remain inaccessible, hindering progress in various aspects. The advantages of maintaining good credit encompass a spectrum of benefits, including easier access to personal loans, increased negotiating leverage, eligibility for insurance discounts, lower interest rates, and streamlined approval processes for business loans, all of which are instrumental in advancing personal and professional endeavors, to mention a few. Additionally, keeping debts paid down will also improve your credit ratings and will increase equity in your investments.

- Notate your credit score on the appointed line (online apps such as *Credit Karma* can help you obtain and monitor your credit score free of charge)

- Under the Debt column, notate all of your debts

- Under the Amount column, notate the amount of each debt

- Calculate your total debt and put that figure on the appropriate line

- Take a moment to think of where you would like to be in 12-weeks in regard to your credit and your debt. When you have reached a reasonable decision, notate it in the appropriate place

CREDIT AND DEBT

Credit Score
735

Debt	Amount
Mortgage	250.000
Capital One	1.500
American Express	12.000
Personal Loan	800
Total Debt:	$264.300

12-week Financial Destination
I plan to pay off my personal loan. my capital one card. and increase my credit score by 20 points.

Example

If you find yourself grappling with debt and facing challenges in managing your finances, it is advisable to consider consulting a financial planner.

MONTHLY CALENDAR

    While no plans are ever guaranteed, maintaining a flexible attitude is essential. However, it's equally important to create plans and set timelines for our goals; otherwise, they might remain unaccomplished. This is why having a clear view of each day in a month proves beneficial in steering us towards achieving our objectives and assuring that no events or appointments are in conflict or forgotten.

MONTH: _____			
Sunday	Monday	Tuesday	Wednesday
		1	2
photoshoot 6	7	VAC 8	9
		Lunch with Jill 15	16
13	14		
	Dr. Appt 8:00 21	22	23
20			
27	28	29	30

NOTES:_____
_____
_____

YEAR: _____		
Thursday	Friday	Saturday
3	4	*soccer game* 5
ATION 10	11	12
Finish first 3 chapters 17	18	19
24	Nio's BDAY! 25	26
31		

"AN HOUR OF PLANNING CAN SAVE YOU TEN HOURS OF DOING" –DALE CARNEGIE

NOTES:_____
Take more naps
Make sure that the kids get to practice on time!

Example

- Fill out the month and year at the top of your monthly calendar

- Enter the dates in each designated box as illustrated (ensure the first date aligns with the correct day of the week). You may need to refer to a different calendar to acquire this information, as these inserts are not specific to one particular year.

- Enter any important events that take place during that month in the appropriate date perhaps even highlighting very important dates to assure they don't get overlooked

- In the notes portion at the bottom of the calendar add any bits of helpful information to help you throughout your month

YOUR WEEK AT A GLANCE

Weekly schedules serve as a powerful tool to visualize and actualize your short-term goals. They ensure effective time and energy management, enabling you to optimize your efforts efficiently.

WEEK AT A GLANCE

Sunday	• clean out garage • deep clean bathroom
Monday	• work 9 - 5 • exercise • pick up dry-cleaning
Tuesday	• Work 9-4 • exercise • Joey Soccer 6 • pick up dinner
Wednesday	• work 9- 5 • cardio kickboxing • pick up John's rx • Bible Study 7

"You must be the change you wish to see in the world."
-Mahatma Gandhi

FROM: start date of week TO: end date of week

Thursday	• exercise • work 9 - 3 • Cancel subscription • Joey soccer 6
Friday	• exercise • work 9 -5 • Meet girls for dinner
Saturday	• Church • catch the matinee

MY WEEKLY INSPIRING QUOTE:
Focus on the good in everyone!!!

Example

- At the top right side, enter the start date of the week and the end date of the week

- Allocate tasks and activities according to each day on the schedule, ensuring a balanced workload without overburdening yourself.

- For each week, challenge yourself to create an inspiring quote or mantra that you can remind yourself of throughout the week and input it on the bottom of the right page in your planner.

Your Weekly Objectives for each Role

Remember that true success can only be attained if you are devoting time to improving the various roles each week. Augment your role as captain by engaging in activities that will enrich your mind and spirit. Improve and maintain your vessel by nourishing your body and excelling in your work.

Encourage and nurture your crew by spending time with loved ones and cultivating your interpersonal relationships. Inspire the Portmen by informing them of the helpful products and services you have to offer and sharing with them your time and/ or resources.

- Take a few moments and think about ways you can improve each role then list them in the spaces provided

- List the Value Activites and other activities you would like to or need to accomplish that week in the bottom section of the page

WEEKLY OBJECTIVES

CAPTAIN
- meditate
- suduko puzzles
- Church
- meet with therapist

VESSEL
- exercise
- work at day job
- eat a healthy diet
- get hair done

CREW
- go to Aden's soccer game
- Help Aden with homework
- Have date night with hubby
- Ask your boss how you can better assist

PORTMEN
- specify what target audience needs
- research effective advertising
- volunteer at soup kitchen
- drop clothes off at Goodwill

- finish writing chap. 1
- set up website
- rake leaves
- set up instgram account

Example

Your Weekly Meal plan

This segment of your planner holds the key to significantly reducing your expenses and stress levels, while simultaneously enhancing your overall health and wellness. Failing to plan our meals for the week often leads to squandering valuable time and money through unnecessary store trips and the purchase of unhealthy, unneeded items.

Conversely, by strategizing your meals for the week, you can streamline store visits to just once, exclusively purchase essential items, and guarantee a week filled with delicious, healthful meals. This proactive approach eliminates the stress of pondering what to prepare for dinner each night.

Some people even prefer to allocate one day of the week for meal prepping. This not only liberates a significant portion of your schedule, allowing you to focus more intently on your projects, but it also guarantees a steady supply of nutritious and readily available meals throughout each day.

Weekly Meal Plan

Sunday
B: Oatmeal
L: Turkey Sandwich
D: Salmon and Asparagus
S: Celery sticks and PB

Monday
B: Fasting
L:
D:
S:

Tuesday
B: Yogurt and Toast
L: Ramen
D: Tostadas
S: Hummus andc carrots

Wednesday
B: Protein Smoothie
L: Salad
D: Grilled Chicken
S: Apples and PB

Thursday
B: Cereal
L: Salad
D: Spaghetti
S: Spring Rolls

Friday
B: Oatmeal
L: Protein Bar
D: EAT OUT :)
S: Chips and Salsa

Saturday
B: Bagel
L: Vege Burrito
D: Salmon and potatos
S: Fruit bowl

Health Concerns
HIGH CHOLESTEROL

Grocery List
Lettuce	TP
Tomatos	garbage bags
Chips	potatoes
salsa	cucumbers
noodles	
apples	
salmon	
Oatmeal	
PB	

Example

- Think of delicious, not-too-difficult-to-preapare meals and snacks that you can have for each day. List them on the appropriate spaces (B- Breakfast, L- Lunch, D- Dinner, S- Snack)

- List any of your and/or your family members' health concerns at the bottom left side of the page as a reminder to plan meals that will help and not harm such conditions

- Add the items needed to prepare the meals as well as other essential items on your Grocery List

> In the back of your planner, you will find a section where you can add your favorite go-to meals along with their recipes. I enjoy a good vegetable stir-fry. How about you?

Your Weekly Exercise plan

Consistent engagement in physical activity has been extensively demonstrated to be effective in both preventing and managing noncommunicable diseases including heart disease, stroke, diabetes, and various types of cancers. Additionally, it plays a vital role in averting hypertension, sustaining a healthy body weight, and fostering improvements in mental health, overall quality of life, and well-being.

Although a veritable fountain of youth may not exist, exercise reigns as the foremost factor in preserving both a youthful appearance and mindset. Moreover, it serves as a potent defense against cognitive decline while substantially enhancing confidence across all aspects of life. This pivotal role underscores the significance of incorporating exercise into your daily routine.

Weekly Exercise Log

	Cardio	Upper Body	Lower Body	Core
Sunday				
Monday	45 min Stair Climber	-Rows -Curls		-Planks -Sit ups
Tuesday	-45 min treadmill		-Leg Press -Leg ext -leg curls	-Planks -Sit ups
Wednesday	Cardio Kickboxing			
Thursday	45 min Stair Climber	-Rows -Curls		-Planks -Sit ups
Friday	-45 min treadmill		-Leg Press -Leg ext -leg curls	-Planks -Sit ups
Saturday				

Weight Gain/Loss

138/ down 10 pounds!!!

Example

- It may be necessary to speak with a personal trainer about the best workout plan for you as they will consider your goals as well as your physical limitations

- Once you have a good exercise plan together, input it in the appropriate boxes

- At the bottom of the page, input your starting weight, current weight and losses or gains if you have chosen to keep track of it

HOURLY SCHEDULE AND DAILY OBJECTIVES

Having an hourly schedule allows for better planning and helps you make the most of your time. It also provides a visual representation of how your time is spent, making it easier to identify patterns, optimize efficiency, and make adjustments as needed.

DAILY SCHEDULER

DATE: Today's Date

AM	
5 AM	exercise/ walk dogs
6 AM	fold laundry
7 AM	meditate
	work on book
8 AM	
9 AM	work
10 AM	
11 AM	
12 PM	lunch/ nap
1 PM	work
2 PM	
3 PM	
4 PM	
5 PM	relax/ hot tub
	help Aden with homework
6 PM	Dinner -Spaghetti Bolognese
7 PM	
8 PM	Work on book
9 PM	
10 PM	Bed time :)

DAILY OBJECTIVES

1. Call plumber
2. Schedule teeth-clean
3. post promo stuff
4. research medical terms
5. pick up rx

6. pay water bill
7. call travel agent
8.
9.
10.

Your Daily Objectives represent a set of activities slated for completion within a single day. Often, we tend to be overly ambitious when crafting this section of our planner, loading it with an abundance of tasks. It's crucial not to be too hard on yourself if you're unable to tick off every item on the list in a day.

Focus on addressing the most pivotal tasks and highlight them if possible. Once each task is accomplished, mark them off. For unfinished tasks, seamlessly transfer them to the next day's list. Ideally, by week's end, you'll have successfully completed all these objectives.

- Think about your various roles, your ports of call, and your value activities before making your list of daily objectives

- Write your daily objectives on the allocated lines

Mastering time management can be a challenging endeavor. If you desire expert guidance to effectively learn the art of time management, simply scan the QR code for professional assistance.

BELIEVE AND YOU WILL ACHIEVE

T ake a much-deserved deep, cleansing breath now and say aloud, "Through planning and believing, I will soon be achieving!" Pronouncing these words has now infused your intention into the ether, forging connections with thoughts aligned with this positive mindset.

Rest assured that by adhering to the steps outlined in this guidebook, you will successfully attain all your goals. Nevertheless, it is crucial to prioritize self-care. While this may appear simple for some, driven individuals may find it challenging to permit themselves complete relaxation, both physically and mentally.

Allocate a specific day each week dedicated not only to easing the tension in your body but also to calming your mind. Ironically, taking a break from actively pursuing your goals can paradoxically contribute to their achievement. Some of our most profound insights emerge not during moments of busyness but in stillness when we are receptive to the Divine voice.

Furthermore, refrain from being too hard on yourself if you don't accomplish all your goals within the 12 weeks. It's possible that your aspirations were overly ambitious, or unforeseen and more pressing matters may have diverted your attention from pursuing your goals entirely. Life is unpredictable and maintaining a flexible mindset is important. You can always start the process over.

It is also important to allocate your time accordingly. Abraham Lincoln wisely remarked, "Give me six hours to chop down a tree and I'll spend the first four sharpening the axe" This insightful advice underscores the significance of proper preparation and planning. Indeed, neglecting meticulous planning can lead to not only hours but potentially days, weeks, or even months of squandered time.

Select a designated day to plan your week, taking into account the optimal and most efficient utilization of your time. Additionally, give careful thought to activities that can be delegated. Delegation is a pivotal aspect of achieving success and entrusting less critical tasks to others is a wise practice. Consider extending responsibilities to your children as well; involving them in certain tasks will develop a sense of responsibility and contribute to their personal development.

You may find that the absence of constant busyness may create a sense of unease, as you adjust to the newfound clarity and control over your time. Much like when the chaos of a bustling household suddenly quiets down when children leave home, the transition to a more organized and goal-oriented schedule can initially feel unfamiliar. This phase of adjustment is a natural part of the process. It's an opportunity for you to embrace the peace that comes with effective planning and use it as a canvas for new pursuits, personal growth, or simply enjoying moments of tranquility.

Your *12-Weeks to Success* planner will be your most invaluable tool on your journey to success. Enriched with resources for cultivating a successful mindset, it effortlessly provides the practical elements essential for your endeavors. View it not just as a map but also as your compass, guaranteeing you stay on the right course and navigate towards your goals with unwavering precision. Once you reach your destination, imagine a new one and let the adventures continue!

Your destination awaits you!

ABOUT THE AUTHOR

Dawn M. Richey, a multifaceted individual, has led a remarkable journey marked by her roles as a mother, author, ordained Christian minister, Subconscious Behavioral Therapist, Life Coach, and Nashville recording artist.

Born in Palm Desert, California, Dawn's early years were shaped by humble beginnings. In her early 20s, she dedicated herself to the fitness industry, working as a personal fitness trainer. However, her passion for music drew her eastward to Nashville, where she thrived as a professional bass player and songwriter for a small publishing company.

In the heart of Music City, Dawn embarked on a spiritual journey by founding the Association of Soul Savers, a ministry purposed to spread the Gospel of Jesus Christ. As she gained traction as a minister and solo artist, a pivotal moment occurred when she became pregnant. Faced with the challenge of balancing a music career and motherhood, she opted for stability. She decided to pursue her love for helping and healing people by becoming a therapist.

Resuming her education, Dawn earned her bachelor's degree in psychology. However, a serendipitous encounter with a family friend who overcame chronic migraine headaches through subconscious therapy changed the course of her life. Inspired, she studied under the guidance of George Kappas while running a successful housekeeping business to support herself and her newborn son.

With the help of the Mental Bank program, she doubled her income within a year and the following year doubled it again when she sold her housekeeping business so she could focus on her own subconscious therapy and life coaching practice. It soon began thriving as she collaborated with top doctors and surgeons from Vanderbilt University, helping patients with symptoms resistant to traditional medical procedures and difficulties adhering to critical diet plans. Notably, she facilitated the remarkable recovery of a woman who had been unable to walk for over a decade through subconscious reprogramming and prayer.

As the years passed, however, despite her success in aiding others to overcome their challenges and attain their aspirations, an underlying dissatisfaction emerged as her own goals remained unmet. She struggled to meet the demands of motherhood and juggle all her various responsibilities. Amid this demanding reality, the idea of undertaking ambitious projects, such as writing a book, reinventing her ministry, and completing an album she had envisioned for so long, seemed nearly impossible.

Rather than give up, Dawn confronted the challenge head-on, determined to find a way to weave these creative pursuits into the fabric of her busy life. She knew that time management and meticulous planning would be imperative and that if she could create a planner to help her achieve these tasks, then her clients could also benefit from it.

In her quest to transform dreams into reality, she set a bold yet achievable timeframe of 12 weeks to accomplish the monumental tasks of writing a book, producing an album, and reinventing her ministry—all while managing her daily responsibilities, personal health, and homeschooling her son. Recognizing the importance of giving her aspirations a tangible structure, Dawn embraced the wisdom that a goal without a deadline is merely a dream.

Little did Dawn anticipate that creating a planner to facilitate this ambitious timeline would prove to be a demanding task in itself. The irony of needing a planner to organize the process of creating her planner added a touch of humor to the challenge.

As always, through prayer and silent contemplation, she was divinely guided to create the planner you are now using yourself and upon its completion, utilized the methods therein to reach her cherished goals. She carefully cut back on her office hours and delegated non-essential tasks so she could focus on reaching all her Ports of Call. Every night before bed, she would look at her vision board, read her mission statement,10-year goal, and 12-week goal, and she would complete her Prosperity Bank Ledger. She also made sure to give daily attention to all of her various roles and used self-hypnosis to augment her motivation.

As a happy ending would have it, not only did she finish her book, but she completed her album, reinvented her ministry, and reached her weight-loss goal of 15 pounds all within 12 weeks! Upon completion of each 12-week program, she begins a new one with new goals and refined destinations. The happy ending to her narrative is a celebration of determination, creativity, and the transformative potential inherent within each of us!

Whether through her ministry, life coaching, or other endeavors, she continues to share the principles of strategic planning, determination, and the integration of spirituality to help individuals reawaken their dreams and turn them into tangible realities.

If you've enjoyed this book, please consider leaving a review.

www.ingramcontent.com/pod-product-compliance
Lightning Source LLC
LaVergne TN
LVHW010031070426
835508LV00005B/292